The Sinking of the USS *Indianapolis*: The Harrowing Story of One of the U.S. Navy's Deadliest Incidents during World War II

By Charles River Editors

The USS *Indianapolis* at Pearl Harbor in 1937

About Charles River Editors

Charles River Editors provides superior editing and original writing services across the digital publishing industry, with the expertise to create digital content for publishers across a vast range of subject matter. In addition to providing original digital content for third party publishers, we also republish civilization's greatest literary works, bringing them to new generations of readers via ebooks.

Sign up here to receive updates about free books as we publish them, and visit Our Kindle Author Page to browse today's free promotions and our most recently published Kindle titles.

Introduction

The USS *Indianapolis* in 1939

The Sinking of the USS *Indianapolis* (July 30, 1945)

"I awoke. I was in the air. I saw a bright light before I felt the concussion of the explosion that threw me up in the air almost to the overhead. A torpedo had detonated under my room. I hit the edge of the bunk, hit the deck, and stood up. Then the second explosion knocked me down again. As I landed on the deck I thought, 'I've got to get the hell out of here!'" – Dr. Lewis Haynes

The United States lost hundreds of ships during the course of World War II, from the deadly explosion of the USS *Arizona* during the attack on Pearl Harbor to the sinking of John F. Kennedy's PT-109, a patrol boat with a crew of less than 15. However, few of the ships lost in the Pacific suffered a fate as gripping or tragic as the sinking of the heavy cruiser USS *Indianapolis* on July 30, 1945.

The USS *Indianapolis* had been launched nearly 15 years earlier, and it had already survived kamikaze attacks while fighting the Japanese. In July 1945, the cruiser and its crew of nearly 1,200 delivered parts for the first atomic bomb to an air base at Tinian, but due to a chain of events and miscommunication, the cruiser veered into the path of a Japanese submarine shortly after midnight on July 30. Torpedo attacks sank the ship within 15 minutes of the encounter, and about 300 men went down with the ship, but unfortunately, the trials and tribulations were just starting for the survivors. After the call to abandon ship and distress signals were sent out, nearly 900 men found themselves in the water, but the Navy remained unaware of the fate of the *Indianapolis*, so the survivors would end up spending over 4 days adrift at sea.

Those who didn't drown had to deal with the effects of dehydration, starvation, and exposure, but while those conditions were terrible enough, the most notorious aspect of the story was the presence of sharks, and the seemingly random nature in which they attacked the sailors. The sailors could never be sure if a gruesome death was coming at any instant, especially at night, and while it's unclear how many men were actually eaten by sharks, salvage efforts eventually found the remains of nearly 60 bodies that indicated they were bitten.

By the time rescue efforts were completed, just 300 men were saved, and the fallout over the episode was intense. To this day, the sinking of the USS *Indianapolis* is controversial, and historians continue to debate who shouldered the most blame for what occurred. *The Sinking of the USS Indianapolis: The Harrowing Story of One of the U.S. Navy's Deadliest Incidents during World War II* chronicles the tragic fate of the ship and everything the survivors had to endure in the aftermath of the sinking. Along with pictures of important people, places, and events, you will learn about the USS *Indianapolis* like never before, in no time at all.

The Sinking of the USS *Indianapolis*: The Harrowing Story of One of the U.S. Navy's Deadliest Incidents during World War II

Chapter 1: Captain McVay Was Not Told

"Our captain requested a destroyer escort to cross the Philippine Sea. He was told an escort was not necessary. His request was denied. He was not told of the sinking of the destroyer escort Underhill by an enemy submarine within range of our path. He was led to believe this transit was safe and told only of unconfirmed submarine sightings. The transit was not safe. He was given orders to zigzag at his discretion. He used his discretion to cease zigzagging at midnight in severely limited visibility…The visibility that night was not good…as all of us know who were there that night…Naval intelligence had broken the Japanese code and knew that the submarine which sank us was within range of our path. Captain McVay was not told…" - Crewman Paul J. Murphy

Of all the things that makes the sinking of the USS *Indianapolis* a compelling and tragic story, the fact that its demise was so closely linked to the end of the war in Pacific is sadly ironic. By the end of July 1945, Americans were weary of war but optimistic. The fighting in Europe had ended in May, and it seemed like something must surely happen soon to end the war in the Pacific. President Roosevelt had died in April, and he had been replaced by someone far less experienced in Harry Truman. Many liked Truman better than Roosevelt, preferring his homespun humor to FDR's more patrician approach, and while it was evident the Allies were winning the war in the Pacific, it was unclear when the Japanese would be defeated.

In fact, Truman himself faced an incredibly difficult decision. Shortly after taking the oath of office, he had been informed that the country now had in its possession a new and terrible device, a nuclear bomb capable of killing untold thousands with a single detonation. At the same time, the use of such a bomb would certainly kill a substantial number of women, children, and other civilians no matter which Japanese city it was used on.

In May 1945, the Americans and Japanese were engaged in an extremely deadly campaign at Okinawa, an island close enough to use for air attacks on the Japanese mainland. Facing kamikaze attacks and fanatic Japanese soldiers, the Allies suffered 50,000 casualties, leading American military officials to estimate upwards of a million Allied casualties if they had to invade the Japanese mainland. Besides, the nuclear bombs being constructed in Los Alamos were always intended to be used in Japan, so the end of the war in Europe did not make the bombs any less necessary.

The bomb was not yet officially complete, nor had it been tested, before President Truman and his advisors were being pelted by letters from scientists raising ethical objections to the use of the nuclear bomb. It was not making Truman's decision any less difficult. The first of such letters came in June 1945 from James Franck, a Jewish escapee from Central Europe who came to the United States and worked on nuclear research. In his letter, Franck offered advice on the threat of a nuclear arms race should the U.S. use the weapon. He suggested that the weapon would be so powerful and so devastating that nations around the world would race to gain access to the technology themselves. Franck's solution was to either keep the nuclear bomb secret indefinitely or to test it in a barren desert before the United Nations, thereby showing Japan and the world its devastating destructiveness. The letter was signed by Franck and other notable nuclear scientists, including Leo Szilárd and Glenn Seaborg, both early proponents of and contributors to the Manhattan Project. The letter was received and taken into account by a nuclear arms committee appointed by President Truman.

Franck

A second important letter came in July, less than a month before the nuclear detonations over Hiroshima and Nagasaki. Penned by Leo Szilárd, the document was signed by an additional 69 physicists and researchers. It explicitly opposed using the weapon against Japan unless that nation was offered surrender terms beforehand and rejected them. All 70 petitioners lost their jobs in the Manhattan Project, though the letter was received by the same committee that reviewed the Franck Letter.

In between the two petitions, the American nuclear bomb had finally come to fruition. On July 16, 1945, the first detonation of a nuclear device took place in Alamogordo, New Mexico. The results of the successful test reached President Truman, who was then attending an Allied Conference in Potsdam, and while there, he presented the news to Soviet leader Joseph Stalin. Stalin feigned surprise; espionage missions had revealed American nuclear research to the Soviets before it had even reached Vice President Truman.

A picture of the test

Before making his decision to use the bomb, Truman considered some of the ethical advice submitted by American physicists. In particular, he took the idea of informing the Japanese beforehand to heart. At the Potsdam Conference on July 26th, Truman, the United Kingdom and China issued the Potsdam Declaration, giving the Japanese an ultimatum to surrender or suffer "prompt and utter destruction."

Japan chose to ignore the ultimatum, and ultimately Truman chose to use the bombs. Truman took the scientists' concerns into account, but the deadly experience of Okinawa made clear that hundreds of thousands of Americans would be casualties in a conventional invasion of the mainland of Japan. Moreover, the fanatical manner in which Japanese soldiers and civilians held out on Okinawa indicated that the Japanese would suffer more casualties during an invasion than they would if the bombs were used. Pursuant to the Quebec Agreement, Canada and Great Britain consented to the use of the bomb. As a result, Truman authorized its use on two sites in Japan.

President Truman ordering the use of the atomic bomb

Even before Truman made his final decision, its potential use required transporting materials to the Pacific so that the bomb could be dropped if necessary. As it turned out, one of the ships carrying parts of the bomb that would be dropped on Hiroshima was the *USS Indianapolis*, a heavy cruiser that was a good choice for such a mission. One of the crewmembers summed up the ship's history before that month: "In World War II the heavy cruiser *USS Indianapolis* earned ten battle stars, including one for its participation in the bombardment of Okinawa in March of 1945 during which it was struck by a kamikaze (suicide plane), resulting in 38 casualties including 12 fatalities. Captain Charles Butler McVay III, a 1920 Naval Academy graduate and career naval officer who had taken command in November of 1944, returned the ship safely to Mare Island in California for repairs."

The *Indianapolis* with a camouflage design in 1944

Photo # NH 53232   USS Indianapolis under fire, off Saipan, June 1944

A picture of the *Indianapolis* fighting in 1944

The *Indianapolis* at Mare Island in July 1945

Naturally, the men aboard the *Indianapolis* were surprised by the cargo they were carrying that month. Captain Lewis L. Haynes, the ship's Chief Medical Officer, explained, "After our repairs were completed, we were supposed to go on our post-repair trial run. But instead, on July 15th, we were ordered to go to San Francisco to take on some cargo. I was amazed to notice that there was a quiet, almost dead Navy Yard. We tied up at the dock there and two big trucks came alongside. The big crate on one truck was put in the port hangar. The other truck had a bunch of men aboard, including two Army officers, CAPT [James F.] Nolan and MAJ [Robert R.] Furman. I found out later that Nolan was a medical officer. I don't know what his job was, probably to monitor radiation. The two men carried a canister, about 3 feet by 4 feet tall, up to ADM Spruance's cabin where they welded it to the deck. Later on, I found out that this held the nuclear ingredients for the bomb and the large box in the hangar contained the device for firing the bomb. And I had that thing welded to the deck above me for 10 days!"

Obviously, the men were curious about what was going on, but given the secretive nature of the bomb, they weren't told much. Haynes remembered, "As we got under way on July 16th, CAPT McVay told his staff we were on a special mission. 'I can't tell you what the mission is. I don't know myself but I've been told that every day we take off the trip is a day off the war.' CAPT McVay told us his orders were that if we had an 'abandon ship,' what was in the admiral's cabin was to be placed in a boat before anybody else. We had all kinds of guesses as to what the cargo was. After refueling at an eerily quiet Pearl Harbor, we made a straight run to Tinian at as much speed as they could economically go, about 25 or 26 knots. Everybody was at Condition Able which was 4 hours on and 4 hours off. It was like going into battle the whole way out. The trip from San Francisco to Tinian took a total of 10 days. When we unloaded our special cargo at Tinian I noticed a couple of general Air Force officers handling these crates like they were a bunch of stevedores. I was even more sure we had something important. We were then ordered to the Philippines for training exercises preparing for the invasion of Kyushu. CAPT McVay asked for an escort, but was told we didn't need one as it was supposedly safe to go to the Philippines. What he wasn't told was that there were Japanese submarines along the way and that Naval Intelligence knew it."

Captain Charles McVay III

If the officers knew little about what was happening, the enlisted men knew less, but that did not stop them from doing their duty, in this case with remarkable effectiveness. Seaman L. D. Cox remembered, "We made it in nine steaming days and that's still the record for a surface vessel. We didn't know what was in the box. ... They also brought another, smaller metal container on board, and carried it up to the Captain's quarters and welded it to the deck. That wasn't common knowledge with the crew at the time, but we knew about it later after we took off. We think that was the uranium part of the bomb. ... My favorite story was that it was a big box of scented toilet paper for General McArthur. Of course we had no way of knowing how serious it was. ... After we left the bomb at Tinian we came back to Guam, and took on supplies. We were told to join the battleship U.S.S. Idaho, in the Philippines for gunnery practice."

In a press release issued in February 1946, about seven months after the tragedy, the Navy claimed, "On July 27, Captain C.B. McVay, III, U.S.N., commanding officer of the Indianapolis, visited the Office of the Port Director, Guam in connection with his routing to Leyte. Later that day the Navigator of the Indianapolis also visited the Port Director's office to obtain the Routing Instructions and discuss their details. Information of possible enemy submarines along the route was contained in the routing instructions and was discussed with the Navigator. The route over which the Indianapolis was to travel, which was the only direct route between Guam and Leyte, and was the route regularly assigned vessels making passage between these islands, was considered within the acceptable risk limit for combatant vessels. Circuitous routes were available from Guam to Leyte, but no special apprehension was felt regarding the use of the direct route by the Indianapolis and no other route was considered. The speed of advance of the Indianapolis (15.7 knots) was set by Captain McVay and was based upon his desire to arrive off the entrance to Leyte Gulf at daylight on July 31 in order to conduct antiaircraft practice prior to his entering the Gulf. To have arrived a day earlier would have required a speed of advance of about 24 knots. No special consideration was given the possibility of delaying the departure of the ship from Guam in order to enable her to proceed in company with other vessels, since the route assigned was not thought by the Port Director to be unduly hazardous. Zigzagging was, by his routing instructions, left to the discretion of Captain McVay. However, tactical orders then in force required zigzagging in conditions of good visibility, in waters where enemy submarines might be present."

However, crewman Paul J. Murphy noted that McVay and the *Indianapolis* had not been fully informed by the Navy of the danger in their path. "The Indianapolis was then routed to Guam enroute to Leyte. Hostilities in this part of the Pacific had long ceased. The Japanese surface fleet no longer existed as a threat, and 1,000 miles to the north preparations were underway for the invasion of the Japanese mainland. These conditions resulted in a relaxed state of alert at Guam on the part of those who routed the Indianapolis across the Philippine Sea. Although naval authorities at Guam knew that on July 24, four days before the Indianapolis departed for Leyte, the destroyer escort USS Underhill had been sunk by a submarine within range of the path of the our ship, McVay was not told. Further, although a code-breaking system called ULTRA had alerted naval intelligence that a Japanese submarine (the 1-58 by name which ultimately sank the Indianapolis) was operating in our path, McVay was not told."

Chapter 2: What in the Hell is Goin' On?

"Sunday, the 29th of July was a quiet day. The sea was runnin' five or six feet waves, just a beautiful day out. Didn't do too much, read a book, did a little tinkerin' as usual. Had the 8:00 to 12:00 watch and just got off at midnight. A guy relieved me about a quarter to twelve. I went down through the galley and had a cup of coffee. Then went to my compartment and got a blanket off my bed and went back up on deck. I slept under the overhang on the first turret. My battle station was inside it so in case general quarters sounded, I slept underneath it. Just got laid down good, using my shoes for a pillow as usual and the first torpedo hit. I was up and down between the deck and the overhang of the turret like Yankee Doodle Dandy. And, I wondered, "what in the hell is goin' on?" - Crewman Woody Eugene

It is still unclear why McVey was not warned of the danger he was in, but it clearly wasn't sinister, as the Navy had no reason to place one of its best battleships in unnecessary danger. Instead, as Murphy implied, the war seemed so close to an end that authorities were becoming more lax about the kind of danger the Japanese still posed. Murphy noted, "A Navy directive limited such data only to flag officers (i.e., above Captain McVay's rank). … No capital ships, such as Indianapolis, were equipped with anti-submarine detection devices, and none had made the transit between Guam and Leyte during WW II without a destroyer escort. Captain McVay requested such an escort, but, unaware of the ULTRA report, the routing officer indicated that an escort was not necessary. McVay's request was denied (and by the Surface Operations Officer at Guam who was aware of the ULTRA intelligence but who later testified…that the risk of submarine attack along the Indianapolis's route 'was very slight.'!)"

That said, as the Navy's press release pointed out, "The policy determination with regard to the escorting of vessels in the Western Pacific was the function of the Commander in Chief, Pacific Fleet. This policy, which required the escorting of vessels in some areas but dispensed with escorts for some classes of vessels in others, which were less active, was largely dictated by the limited availability of escort vessels. At the time of the sailing of the Indianapolis, there was a shortage in this regard and escorts were, as a rule, not given combatant vessels which were capable of 'taking care of themselves.' The Indianapolis was considered to be in this class and escort, if furnished her, would have been at the expense of other requirements of greater urgency. At the time of her departure from Guam, the Indianapolis was not at peak efficiency; but she was well organized; her personnel were well disciplined and, in the main, well versed in the performance of their routine duties. Training of personnel was continuing and her visit to Leyte was being made in order to complete her refresher training program."

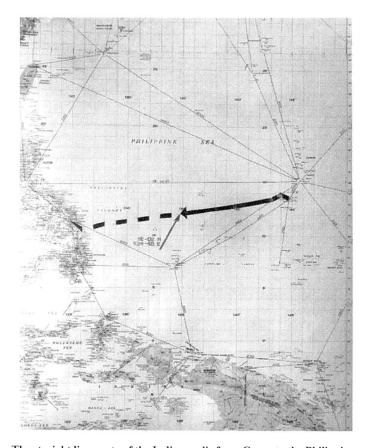

The straight line route of the Indianapolis from Guam to the Philippines

Though the danger was judged to be slight, McVay was under orders to be careful as he sailed across the Pacific that week, and for decades, those seeking to avoid being torpedoed by submarines sailed in a zigzag so as not to present a straight shot. However, McVay was also given a certain amount of discretion in his orders, and this discretion would end up costing him everything. One of the men on board explained, "McVay's orders were to zigzag at his discretion. Before midnight on Sunday, July 29, with visibility severely limited due to cloud cover, McVay issued orders to cease zigzagging and to be notified if there were any changes in the weather, then retired to his cabin. At midnight with clouds breaking on the eastern horizon, the Indianapolis was silhouetted as a blur, heading almost directly toward the 1-58 to the west."

Thus, the evening of July 29th seemed to be like so many others on the *Indianapolis*, and a skeleton night crew stood watch while most of their buddies slept. Cox, one of the men on duty at the time, discussed the events that night from his perspective: "My duties on the bridge were either to steer the ship, to be on the telephone with the engine room, or to be lookout. On this night my assignment was to communicate with the engine room. I took the headphones and about five or ten minutes later there was an explosion - we had been hit by a torpedo. I was blown up into the air about five feet and landed on my stomach. As I started to get to my feet, I looked up and there was debris, water, flames and everything up above me. And the bridge was 81 feet from the waterline - so that shows you how powerful an explosion it was. I started on up and we were hit by another torpedo. This one hit the ammunition magazine. … We didn't know for sure it was a torpedo; we didn't know anything."

Lieutenant Donald Blum was standing watch that night and was one of the few survivors to witness what happened. "I was on watch just after midnight when the ship was hit [by torpedoes fired from the Japanese submarine I-58]. At first I thought it was a boiler exploding because I saw flames shooting up through the stack. We lost communications, and in a few minutes we began to list starboard. I slipped and fell, and when I got up the ship was leaning."

On the other hand, like most of the men, Dr. Haynes was awoken out of a sound sleep by the blast. "On July 29th I was pretty tired because I had given the whole crew cholera shots all day. I remember walking through the warrant officer's quarters and declining to join a poker game as I was so tired. I then went to bed." He was not asleep for long when, "I awoke. I was in the air. I saw a bright light before I felt the concussion of the explosion that threw me up in the air almost to the overhead. A torpedo had detonated under my room. I hit the edge of the bunk, hit the deck, and stood up. Then the second explosion knocked me down again. As I landed on the deck I thought, 'I've got to get the hell out of here!'"

By this time, Woody Eugene and most of the other crewmen who survived the initial explosion were thinking the same thing. "I got out of my blanket and started to roll out from underneath the turret and the other torpedo hit. Another Yankee Doodle deal, all over the place. I started to walk forward to see what I could see and what I seen was about sixty-foot of the bow chopped off, completely gone. Within a minute and a half, maybe two minutes at the most the bow is startin' to do down. It filled up with water that fast. Everything was open below deck and the water just flooded in and we were still under way, just scoopin' water. Complete chaos, total and complete chaos all over the whole ship. Screams like you couldn't believe and nobody knew what was goin' on."

Japanese submarine I-58

I-58's torpedo room

Mochitsura Hashimoto, the commander of I-58

Chapter 3: Death All Around

"SUDDENLY it was all gone: gun, guts, glory. In a matter of moments the tough guys who were so vain, were either dead or shark food. 'WHAM-BOOM' in the middle of the night. A Japanese submarine sent us to the waiting jaws of the sharks. Roughly 800 of us made it into the life jackets to float and bob for five days and nights - roasting in the day time, freezing at nights with no water or food, over 200 miles from land. Men became like animals, would have murdered whoever might have had the water. After 24 hours the wounded died - sharks were everywhere at once - men screaming, groaning, with death all around us for five days and nights without rest. One estimate is that the sharks killed about four an hour. Some drank salt water and died in terrible pain. Others simply cracked up and went mad." - Crewman Tommy Reid

Cox noted that within moments of the first explosion, McVay was on the bridge of the ship and doing whatever he could. "The explosions knocked the Captain out of his bunk and he came up and took charge. I was told to get him a lifejacket and so I got one and helped him into it. All power was out. … By this time we were laying down on our right side at such a degree that you could nearly walk down the smoke stack. The Captain said to pass the word to abandon ship. I took him at his word. I had heard how a ship when it sinks can suck you down and under. And I had also heard that a lot of times that a captain will go down with his ship - and I was with

Captain McVay, so when he said 'Abandon Ship', I left him."

Others, like Haynes, were already preparing to make for the water. He later remembered, "I grabbed my life jacket and started to go out the door. My room was already on fire. I emerged to see my neighbor Ken Stout. He said, 'Let's go,' and stepped ahead of me into the main passageway. I was very close to him when he yelled, 'Look out!' and threw his hands up. I lifted the life jacket in front of my face, and stepped back. As I did, a wall of fire went 'Whoosh!' It burned my hair off, burned my face, and the back of my hands. That's the last I saw of Ken."

Moving on quickly toward the nearest exit, Haynes described the next few moments in excruciating detail: "I started out trying to go to the forward ladder to go up on the fo'c'sle deck. There was a lot of fire coming up through the deck right in front of the dentist's room. That's when I realized I couldn't go forward and turned to go aft. As I did, I slipped and fell, landing on my hands. I got third degree burns on my hands -- my palms and all the tips of my fingers. I still have the scars. I was barefooted and the soles of my feet were burned off. Then I turned aft to go back through the wardroom. I would have to go through the wardroom and down a long passageway to the quarterdeck, but there was a terrible hazy smoke with a peculiar odor. I couldn't breathe and got lost in the wardroom. I kept bumping into furniture and finally fell into this big easy chair. I felt so comfortable. I knew I was dying but I really didn't care."

Fortunately, all his years of medical training snapped him out of his potentially deadly complacence when he was confronted with someone else in need. "Then someone standing over me said, 'My God, I'm fainting!' and he fell on me. Evidently that gave me a shot of adrenalin and I forced my way up and out. Somebody was yelling, 'Open a porthole!' All power was out and it was just a red haze. The ship was beginning to list and I moved to that side of the ship. I found a porthole already open. Two other guys had gone out through it. I stuck my head out the porthole, gulping in some air, and found they had left a rope dangling. I looked down to see water rushing into the ship beneath me. I thought about going out the porthole into the ocean but I knew I couldn't go in there. Instead I grabbed the rope which was attached to an overhanging floater net. I pulled myself through the porthole and up to the deck above. I then went to my battle station, which was the port hangar. My chief, [CPhM John A.] Shmueck, and a lot of casualties were back there. I think the moon was going in and out because at times I could see clearly, other times not. We were trying to put dressings and give morphine to badly burned men when an officer came up and said, 'Doctor, you'd better get life jackets on your patients.'"

Obviously, these were ominous words, given that nobody would prepare to take injured men into the water while there was any hope left that the ship might stay afloat. Obeying orders, the doctors prepared for the worst. "So Shmueck and I went up a ladder to the deck above where there were some life jackets. We got a whole bunch of life jackets and went back down and started to put them on the patients. I remember helping a warrant officer. His skin was hanging in shreds and he was yelling, 'Don't touch me, don't touch me.' I kept telling him we had to get the jacket on. I was putting the jacket on when the ship tipped right over. He just slid away from me. The patients and the plane on the catapult all went down in a big, tangling crash to the other side. I grabbed the lifeline and climbed through to avoid falling. And by the time I did, the ship was on its side. Those men probably all died as the plane came down on top of them. All the rescue gear and everything we had out went down, patients and everything together."

Once the survivors had done everything they could, those who were still well enough to move began to abandon ship. Blum was among the first in the water: "My watch station was about 60 feet up and I saw water a few feet from me. I prepared to jump. Training taught me to swim away so I would not get caught in any suction. I swam as far as I could on one breath, and when I looked again, I saw a propeller coming down on me, still turning. I became a motivated swimmer, and the next time I looked the ship was gone. Here I was, alone, in the middle of the ocean without a life jacket, in the pitch-black darkness. I thought I would wake up in my bunk, dry, having had a bad dream. I swam about an hour and finally found two sailors with a preserver."

Crewman Zeb Wilcox of Texas had a similarly harrowing story: "About midnight I was relieved of duty and made my way to the deck to lay down, when there was a tremendous explosion and fire came out of the forward starboard and port passageways, extending half the distance of the quarterdeck. We had been hit by 2 Japanese torpedoes and the ship was listing badly, so I grabbed my life jacket and literally stepped off the side of the ship into the water. I quickly swam about 50 feet away and donned my 'Mae West' jacket. The ship, all 615 feet of her, sank within 15 minutes of being hit".

Those who could tried to bring along some of their weaker comrades, and others whispered a quick prayer or sought to comfort men they had already shared so much danger with already. Woody Eugene remembered, "The word got passed down, 'ABANDON SHIP'! It was maybe five minutes and we were really down in the water so we proceeded to abandon ship. Jim Newhall and I went over the side holding hands. I got tangled up in the life line long side the ship. I got untangled and surfaced. I'm all alone so I swam out away from the ship, probably fifty yards, maybe one hundred yards, I don't know. I flipped over on my back and looked back and about two thirds of the ship was in the water, bow first and leanin' to the right, the propellers were still turning. In the silhouette of the sinking ship I could see guys jumpin' off the fantail like crazy. I went over the side with a life jacket. I pulled it off and gave it to one of the younger officers that was screamin' his head off that he didn't have one. Anyway, there I am layin' on my back lookin' at that and no life jacket. I don't hear anybody around me any place so I'm just kind of floatin' and relaxin' when low and behold, a potato crate floats by. Potatoes were packaged in wooded crates then. It was just an empty potato crate, made a good buoyancy to hold on to. Works as good as a life jacket I guess. Then pretty soon I heard some voices. I yelled and who answers me, my buddy Jim Newhall. So I swam over to where he was and there was quite a group of them. It's chaos and everybody talkin' and a lot of the guys were wounded, burned and we were trying to do the best we could."

It was bad enough that the *Indianapolis* had been sunk so quickly, but unbeknownst to the survivors who had abandoned ship, no help would be forthcoming anytime soon. One of the crewmen later noted ruefully, "Once detected, our ship was easily tracked and hit by two torpedoes, sinking in about twelve minutes but leaving time for distress signals, several of which were later said to have been received. But they were each ignored. Shortly afterwards a message was intercepted from the I-58, claiming that it had sunk an American battleship. Although giving no location for the sinking, the message had been sent from the general area through which the Indianapolis was routed. And that message was ignored."

In fact, the *Indianapolis* had gotten off three distress signals, and they were received but not acted upon for various reasons. One commanding officer was drunk at the time, while another had told his men not to bother him. A third officer decided against responding to the distress signal for fear it was the work of the Japanese, who might be trying to trick responding ships into a trap. The fact that the distress signals was even received remained classified for decades, and until those records were made public, the Navy denied that the *Indianapolis* had even sent a single one.

Chapter 4: Nothing I Could Do

"There was nothing I could do but give advice, bury the dead, save the life jackets, and try to keep the men from drinking the salt water when we drifted out of the fuel oil. When the hot sun came out and we were in this crystal clear water, you were so thirsty you couldn't believe it wasn't good enough to drink. I had a hard time convincing the men that they shouldn't drink. The real young ones -- you take away their hope, you take away their water and food -- they would drink salt water and then would go fast. I can remember striking men who were drinking water to try and stop them. They would get diarrhea, then get more dehydrated, then become very maniacal. In the beginning, we tried to hold them and support them while they were thrashing around. And then we found we were losing a good man to get rid of one who had been bad and drank. As terrible as it may sound, towards the end when they did this, we shoved them away from the pack because we had to." - Dr. Lewis Haynes

As the *Indianapolis* continued to list, getting away from the sinking ship became a matter of increased urgency. Cox explained the different kinds of danger confronting the men in the water: "I ran to the port side, the uphill side. I had to reach over and grab a hook and then swing out over the main deck and hit the deck and then the water. It was about 40 feet from where I swung out. I had swallowed a bunch of oil and water and I began to vomit. I swam as fast as I could to get away from the ship; I was still worried about the suction. When I looked back I saw the ship had already laid completely over on her side and the stern was coming up and it just went straight down. You could see the propellers still slowly turning and men still jumping off. It only took 12 minutes for the ship to sink and it was 610 feet long."

Haynes had remained calm during his final moments on the ship, but when he was in the water, he had to fight back his panic. "I slowly walked down the side of the ship. Another kid came and said he didn't have a jacket. I had an extra jacket and he put it on. We both jumped into the water which was covered with fuel oil. I wasn't alone in the water. The hull was covered with people climbing down. I didn't want to get sucked down with the ship so I kicked my feet to get away. And then the ship rose up high. I thought it was going to come down and crush me. The ship kept leaning out away from me, the aft end rising up and leaning over as it stood up on its nose. The ship was still going forward at probably 3 or 4 knots. When it finally sank, it was over a hundred yards from me. Most of the survivors were strung out anywhere from half a mile to a mile behind the ship."

With the ship gone so suddenly, the men were left in eerie silence and now had a moment to process what had just happened. As Haynes observed, everything had happened so fast that it was nearly impossible for the survivors to comprehend the turn of events. "Suddenly the ship was gone and it was very quiet. It had only been 12 minutes since the torpedoes hit. We started to gather together. Being in the water wasn't an unpleasant experience except that the black fuel oil got in your nose and eyes. We all looked the same, black oil all over -- white eyes and red mouths."

However, once the cries of the wounded went up, Haynes' medical training again brought him back to reality. "You couldn't tell the doctor from the boot seamen. Soon everyone had swallowed fuel oil and gotten sick. Then everyone began vomiting. At that time, I could have hidden but somebody yelled, 'Is the doctor there?' And I made myself known. From that point on -- and that's probably why I'm here today -- I was kept so busy I had to keep going. But without any equipment, from that point on I became a coroner. A lot of men were without life jackets. The kapok life jacket is designed with a space in the back. Those who had life jackets that were injured, you could put your arm through that space and pull them up on your hip and keep them out of the water. And the men were very good about doing this, Furthermore, those with jackets supported men without jackets. They held on the back of them, put their arms through there and held on floating in tandem."

Chapter 5: When Daylight Came

"When daylight came we were cold and shivering. We figured we'd be found pretty quick, that people would be looking for us - so all that day we had pretty high hopes. ... It got so hot on us - that the sun was just blistering. Oh, it was so hot. We prayed for darkness. When darkness came we got chilled and began to shake. The water was so cold. Then we prayed for the sun. We had oil all over us. Some people say that the oil helped us, and I guess it did, but when the sun would beat down on you like that, you nearly fried. It was a terrible ordeal. ... We saw sharks from day one, but after a short while they became aggressive. ... We'd hear them scream, and then the water would turn red - they were getting us. A shark got one of my buddies who was just a couple of feet from me - the shark's tail and the water just covered me up, I was that close. If a shark took a leg, or just bit them, then sometimes they would float back up - some did and some didn't. Of course they were all dead. We'd take their life-jackets and their dog tags." - Crewman L. D. Cox

There was little that could be done in the dark, so the men simply coped the best they could as they floated and waited for the sun to rise. According to Eugene, "The next morning we kind of counted heads the best we could. There was about 150 people in the group. We were scattered around quite a bit. Well this isn't too bad, we thought, we'll be picked up today. They knew we were out here after all we were due in the Philippines this morning at 11:00 so when we don't show they'll know. If they didn't get a message off, but we're sure they got a message off, they'll still know where we are so no sweat, we'll be picked up before the day's over."

Haynes was able to remember more details than most, and he later wrote, "When daylight came we began to get ourselves organized into a group and the leaders began to come out. When first light came we had between three and four hundred men in our group. I would guess that probably seven or eight hundred men made it out of the ship. I began to find the wounded and dead. The only way I could tell they were dead was to put my finger in their eye. If their pupils were dilated and they didn't blink I assumed they were dead. We would then laboriously take off their life jackets and give it to men who didn't have jackets. In the beginning I took off their dog tags, said The Lord's Prayer, and let them go. Eventually, I got such an armful of dog tags I couldn't hold them any longer. Even today, when I try to say The Lord's Prayer or hear it, I simply lose it. Later, when the sun came up the covering of oil was a help. It kept us from burning. But it also reflected off the fuel oil and was like a searchlight in your eyes that you couldn't get away from. So I had all the men tie strips of their clothing around their eyes to keep the sun out."

Meanwhile, some survivors, like Cox, found solace in the presence of a friend. "I swam out a little further and I ran into this sailor, all by himself, and he was one of my best buddies. He had been flash burned and somebody had put a lifejacket on him and put him overboard. - His name was Clifford Josey and he only survived an hour or two. I've been told there were rafts, but I never saw any. When the moon came out, I found a little group of about 30 men and we stayed together."

There were indeed some rafts, and Zeb Wilcox was one of the few survivors lucky enough to get into one, but this brought about other dilemmas. "I saw a life raft and got inside and those of us who were unhurt began giving up our place in the raft to all the injured sailors and Marines. I found a 'floater net' and grabbed onto it to conserve energy. We all voiced concern about our situation and whether an SOS was sent out. The sharks began appearing – they were 6-7 feet long and gray. We had a lot of wounded, folks with broken limbs and burns. We prayed that God would give us strength to get through this ordeal and our lives played out before us, but the most important thing I did was tell myself I was a survivor – then it was okay – I knew I would survive."

Blum had also made it through the night, thanks to a fortunately place life ring, and daylight on the morning of July 30 brought at least a small improvement in his fortunes. "I hung on to it until morning when I spotted a loose life jacket. Some time that afternoon, we saw a small group of sailors with four big life floaters built for about 10 people each. I could not get aboard because there was no room but I tied myself to the group."

Those who had remained optimistic about being rescued during the first day had their hopes dashed as the sun went down. At that point, the men realized that there would be no respite to their misery, only a change in its source. Eugene explained, "So the day passed, night came and it was cold. IT WAS COLD. The next mornin' the sun come up and warmed things up and then it got unbearably hot so you start praying for the sun to go down so you can cool off again. When the sharks showed up, in fact they showed up the afternoon before but I don't know of anybody being bit. Maybe one on the second day but we just know we'll be picked up today. They've got it all organized by now, they'll be out here pretty soon and get us, we all thought. The day wore on and the sharks were around. Come night time and nobody showed up. We had another night of cold, prayin' for the sun to come up. What a long night."

With seemingly no rescue efforts coming anytime soon, it was obvious that the men's only hope for survival lay in staying together as much as possible. Haynes noted, "The second night, which was Monday night, we had all the men put their arms through the life jacket of the man in front of him and we made a big mass so we could stay together. We kept the wounded and those who were sickest in the center of the pack and that was my territory. Some of the men could doze off and sleep for a few minutes. The next day we found a life ring. I could put one very sick man across it to support him."

Tuesday night, July 31, brought even more misery and danger than the previous two put together, as the cold was now literally driving men mad. Haynes mentioned the effects: "The water in that part of the Pacific was warm and good for swimming. But body temperature is over 98 and when you immerse someone up to their chin in that water for a couple of days, you're going to chill him down. So at night we would tie everyone close together to stay warm. But they still had severe chills which led to fever and delirium. On Tuesday night some guy began yelling, 'There's a Jap here and he's trying to kill me.' And then everybody started to fight. They were totally out of their minds. A lot of men were killed that night. A lot of men drowned. Overnight everybody untied themselves and got scattered in all directions. But you couldn't blame the men. It was mass hysteria. You became wary of everyone. Till daylight came, you weren't sure. When we got back together the next day there were a hell of a lot fewer. There were also mass hallucinations. It was amazing how everyone would see the same thing. One would see something, then someone else would see it. One day everyone got in a long line. I said, 'What are you doing?' Someone answered, 'Doctor, there's an island up here just ahead of us. One of us can go ashore at a time and you can get 15 minutes sleep.' They all saw the island. You couldn't convince them otherwise. Even I fought hallucinations off and on, but something always brought me back."

Unfortunately, the sun brought little relief during the day, as its reappearance exacerbated the dehydration that also drove the men mad. Those who couldn't take it any longer began to drink the poisonous saltwater they were floating in, and Eugene described the scene during the day on July 31: "The sun finally did rise and it got warmed up again. Some of the guys been drinkin' salt water by now, and they were goin' berserk. They'd tell you big stories about the Indianapolis is not sunk, its' just right there under the surface. I was just down there and had a drink of water out of the drinkin' fountain and the Geedunk is still open. The geedunk bein' the commissary where you buy ice cream, cigarettes, candy, what have you, 'it's still open' they'd tell ya. 'Come on we'll go get a drink of water', and then 3 or 4 guys would believe this story and go with them. It didn't ever get any cooler in the daytime. In fact, Newhall asked me, he said, 'James, do you think it's' any hotter in hell than it is here?' I said, 'I don't know, Jim, but if it is, I ain't goin'.' We were hungry, thirsty, no water, no food, no sleep, getting dehydrated, water logged and more of the guys were goin' berserk. There was fights goin' on so Jim and I decided to heck with this, we'll get away from this bunch before we get hurt. So he and I kind of drifted off by ourselves. We tied our life jackets together so we'd stay together. Jim was in pretty good shape to begin with, but he was burned like crazy. His hand was burned, he couldn't hold on to anything, couldn't touch anything."

Some of the men had been able to remain optimistic, but this came to an abrupt end by the afternoon of July 31. Wilcox recalled, "The first day was not too bad. We had about a 150 men on the 2 life rafts and several floater nets, but day two was a different story. Men started hallucinating, seeing islands and airplanes, giving everyone false hope. Some got into fights thinking the others were the enemy. A few went underwater and claimed they ate chow or drank fresh water. We started losing men and below us we could see sharks everywhere. By day three, men were losing their minds. Drinking salt water does this to people and they would become combative, swim off and sink – then the sharks would get them".

Cox was afraid of consuming even a small amount of saltwater, to the point that he wouldn't touch food that had been in the water. "A potato floated by, but I was so afraid it had salt water in it that I decided not to eat it. … Men also started saying they knew where there was an island. After a while you really didn't know whether they were off or you were off and there really was an island but I decided to stay put." The decision may have saved his life.

Though only a few men knew it and had access to it, some food and freshwater had been found floating in debris within the wake of the sinking, but according to Blum, no one could figure out how to make use of it. "I know how delirious the others got. I decided I would use as little energy as I could and only worry seriously when I could see no others' faces. The group had a keg of water but it was impossible to drink out of it. It was heavy and, when lifted, one would go underwater. … Some, in their delirious states, would swim away, and others said they were going 'below' to the drinking fountain. Some said they had been to the ice cream stand on the ship."

Chapter 6: Difficulties of an Organization

"The acting Port Director at Tacloban, Leyte, Lieutenant Commander Jules C. Sancho, U.S.N.R., was not aware that the Indianapolis had not arrived as was scheduled and that she should be considered as being overdue. It, however, was his duty in his capacity as Acting Port Director, to keep himself informed of such matters. Lieutenant Stuart B. Gibson, U.S.N.R., the Operations Officer under the Port Director, Tacloban, was the officer who was immediately concerned with the movements of the Indianapolis. The non-arrival of that vessel on schedule was known at once to Lieutenant Gibson who not only failed to investigate the matter but made no immediate report of the fact to his superiors. While not excusing the failure of Lieutenant Commander Sancho and Lieutenant Gibson to use the initiative and ordinary good judgment in this connection which would have been expected of naval officers, this dereliction may be related to the difficulties of an organization which had been brought on by the exceedingly rapid expansion of the Navy to meet its wartime requirements." - Navy Press Release, February 1946

The biggest danger to the men, and the most horrifying, were the sharks that constantly circled the outer edges of their groups. It's believed that they were either tiger sharks or oceanic whitetip sharks, but that obviously made little difference to the men of the *Indianapolis*. Eugene remembered, "The day wore on and the sharks were around, hundreds of them. You'd hear guys scream, especially late in the afternoon. Seemed like the sharks were the worst late in the afternoon than they were during the day. Then they fed at night too. Everything would be quiet and then you'd hear somebody scream and you knew a shark had got him."

An oceanic whitetip shark

Albert Kok's picture of a tiger shark

As if to demonstrate just how random the shark attacks were, and the way in which the sharks ended up posing more danger to some groups of survivors than others, Haynes pointed out that he "saw only one shark. I remember reaching out trying to grab hold of him. I thought maybe it would be food. However, when night came, things would bump against you in the dark or brush against your leg and you would wonder what it was. But honestly, in the entire 110 hours I was in the water I did not see a man attacked by a shark. However, the destroyers that picked up the bodies afterwards found a large number of those bodies. In the report I read 56 bodies were mutilated. Maybe the sharks were satisfied with the dead; they didn't have to bite the living."

One anecdote in support of Haynes' assertion came from Wilcox, who came face to face with sharks and lived to tell the tale. "But on day four, I was awakened when a couple of sharks pulled me underwater. I came up fighting to face two gray sharks staring at me. Both were 10 to 12 feet in length and about 10 feet away from me. I think they were trying to see if I was dead so they could eat me, but I told them 'You don't bother me and I won't bother you.' I realized I had floated away from the group and they were nowhere in sight, but about this time, I saw them in the distance on the far side of the sharks, so I swam between the sharks and they followed me all the way to my friends."

As the hours in the water wore on, some survivors turned to their faith to help them carry on. Tommy Reid remembered, "Thank God, the Lord had a man in the midst of us who knew how to pray. Each dawning he would lead us in the Lord's Prayer. He was a country boy from Kentucky. I prayed will all my heart and, of course, the Lord heard my prayer and knew my heart. However, some of the men only said the prayer just repeating it like it was some kind of good-luck charm. When we would hear a plane, Seaman Underwood led in prayer. As the plane came over and passed on, some men would begin to curse and blaspheme in almost the same breath in which they had been praying. Chills went down my spine in this display of vulgar callousness and irreverence."

Others took a completely different approach, like Lieutenant Blum, who later said, "Out of the original crew of 1199, only 316 survived. How is it I did and so many did not? I firmly believe it was because I didn't think I had anywhere to go--others believed heaven was waiting for them. To survive, I kept thinking I should keep on treading water and waiting. I hope this brings to your attention the will to live as the most important ingredient in a rescue."

Chapter 7: The Doyle Arrived

A picture of survivors brought aboard the USS *Cecil J. Doyle*

"The plane dropped life jackets with canisters of water but the canisters ruptured. Then a PBY [seaplane] showed up and dropped rubber life rafts. We put the sickest people aboard and the others hung around the side. I found a flask of water with a 1-ounce cup. I doled out the water, passing the cup down hand to hand. Not one man cheated and I know how thirsty they were. Towards the end of the day, just before dark, I found a kit for making fresh water out of salt water. I tried to read the instructions, but couldn't make sense of it or get it to work right. My product tasted like salt water and I didn't want to take a chance so I threw it into the ocean. I then went to pieces." - Dr. Lewis Haynes

As it turned out, survivors were finally spotted on August 2, four days after the *Indianapolis* went down, and incredibly, that was how the Navy learned the ship had sunk. According to the Navy, "At 11:25 A.M., August 2, while flying in his assigned sector on a routine search mission, Lieutenant (junior grade) Wilbur C. Gwinn, U.S.N.R., flying a twin engine landplane, sighted an oil slick in position approximately 11-30 north, 133-30 east, approximately 250 miles north of Peleliu. He immediately changed course to investigate and soon sighted a group of about 30 survivors. Dropping a life raft and radio transmitter near the group Lieutenant (junior grade) Gwinn radioed a report that alerted all commands in the area having search and rescue forces under their control. All air and surface units capable of rescue operations were ordered to the scene. Upon receipt of the report, Lieutenant Commander George C. Atteberry, U.S.N.R., took off from his base at Peleliu and arrived on the scene at 2:15 P.M. Upon arrival, Lieutenant Commander Atteberry, assisted by a Navy patrol seaplane which had been enroute to the Philippines and had arrived in the area at 1:45 P.M., conducted a further search, both planes dropping life rafts and rescue equipment near survivors. The first of the rescue forces hurrying to the scene to arrive was a Navy CATALINA patrol seaplane. This plane landed in the water about 5:05 P.M., to afford support to those not in life rafts. Coached by Lieutenant Commander Atteberry, the CATALINA seaplane picked up a total of 58 survivors. This plane was so badly damaged on landing and in rescue operations that it could not take off. However, all the rescued were given elementary first aid and a few hours later transferred to a surface vessel. Later in the afternoon, an Army rescue seaplane, a flight of seven additional large Navy planes, and two Army heavy bombers arrived in the area, conducted intensive searches and dropped large quantities of life rafts and other rescue gear, to all personnel sighted."

Lt. Wilbur C. Gwinn, the pilot
who spotted the survivors
of the U.S.S. Indianapolis.

A picture of Gwinn

Haynes wrote about how fortunate the survivors were to be spotted: "It was Thursday [2 Aug] when the plane spotted us. By then we were in very bad shape. The kapok life jacket becomes waterlogged. It's good for about 48 hours. We sunk lower down in the water and you had to think about keeping your face out of water. I knew we didn't have very long to go. The men were semi-comatose. We were all on the verge of dying when suddenly this plane flew over. I'm here today because someone on that plane had a sore neck. He went to fix the aerial and got a stiff neck and lay down in the blister underneath. While he was rubbing his neck he saw us."

Eugene described what was going through his head as Gwinn's plane appeared: "By this time I would have give my front seat in heaven and walked the rotten log all the way through hell for just one cool drink of water. My mouth was so dry it was like cotton. How I got up enough nerve to take a mouth full of salt water and rinse my mouth out and spit it out I don't know but I did. Did it a couple of times before the mornin' was over. That's probably why I ended up with salt-water ulcers in my throat. When we got picked up my throat was bigger than my head. Anyway, we're out there in the sun prayin' for it to go down again, then low and behold there's a plane. Course there had been planes every day since day one. They were real high and some of the floaters had mirrors that tried to attract them, but nothing. Anyway, this one showed up and flew by and we thought, 'Oh hell, he didn't see us either. He's gone.' Then we seen him turn and come back and we knew we had been spotted. What a relief that was…It was a little PV1 Ventura. It was out on submarine patrol and he spotted us. He radioed back to his base and instead of sending some help out, the Navy sent one plane out. One PBY that came out and circled and radioed back to the base that there was a bunch of people in the water and he needed more assistance and more survival gear."

A PV-1 Ventura

Like the others, Cox was thrilled: "The hair on my head stood straight up, I was so happy. … Later that night there was this bright light shining - it was like a light from heaven. One of the rescue vessels had turned on their flood lights to give us hope."

Although the Navy report didn't specify it in detail, once the information was sent out, a PBY Catalina piloted by Lieutenant R. Adrian Marks alerted the destroyer USS *Cecil J. Doyle*, which ensured that the destroyer would head to the scene and start picking up survivors. Marks had rendered a valuable service merely by alerting the USS *Cecil J. Doyle*, but his subsequent rescue efforts would become the stuff of legends. The Navy reported, "Lt. Adrian Marks PBY-5A was the fourth aircraft on the scene but the first to make any rescues. After dropping 3 rubber rafts and 2 survival kits and after notifying the base of the unexpected magnitude of the rescue job, he decided a landing was necessary. He felt that the survivors located in the rafts or large groups stood the best chance of survival until help from surface craft arrived and that the immediate problem was to get assistance to the singles and to the small groups without rafts who stood a poor chance of survival or of being picked up after darkness set in. Accordingly, at 1705, more than 7 hours before the first rescue vessel, Lt. Marks made a power stall landing amidst 12 foot swells at approximately 11-54N 133-47E and began taxiing among the survivors. LCDR. George C. Atteberry (CO of VPB-152), who was overhead in a PV, assisted by leading the PBY to the singles and small groups. In the 2-1/ 2 hours remaining before darkness, 54 men were taken aboard the plane, given fresh water and limited first aid treatment, and placed either in a compartment or on the wing."

A picture of a PBY Catalina landing

**Lt. R. Adrian Marks with the PBY
he later sacrificed to save
56 survivors of the U.S.S. Indianapolis.**

In fact, Marks was disobeying orders by landing in shark-infested waters, and in discussing Marks' landing, Eugene's description took one of those turns that usually only happened in adventure novels. "The pilot ended up landin' in the water and picked up a lot of guys, the single guys, one or two guys that were together so the afternoon went on. Late in the afternoon before dark there was another PBY on the scene. He dropped his survival gear and he dropped a little three-man rubber raft. Jim and I tried to swim to it. He made it but I didn't. I was just so wore out from holding him up and hangin' on to him all day and the night before, I just couldn't make it but he did. About the time he got on it there was two other guys so there is three of them total in it and that's all it was made for, three. Anyway, the other direction there was two guys in the water and the two guys in the raft told Jim, 'we'll go over there and pick those two up'. Jim said, 'No, we're goin' go pick Woody up then we'll go get those two guys.' They said 'Nope, we're goin' to do it the other way.' The raft contained those little aluminum oars that come in two pieces and Jim put one of them together and threw the other one over board. 'Okay you guys, I don't want to be mean but we're goin' over to get Woody and you guys are goin' to do the paddling by hand. If you don't things are goin' to happen with this oar that you ain't agoin' to like.' So they came over and picked me up and that's how I owe Jim Newhall my life. If it had not been for that I wouldn't be here tellin' this story."

Haynes also wrote about how remarkable Marks' landing was. "I watched the PBY circle and suddenly make an open-sea landing. This took an awful lot of guts. It hit, went back up in the air and splashed down again. I thought he'd crashed but he came taxiing back. I found out later he was taxiing around picking up the singles. If he hadn't done this, I don't think we would have survived. He stayed on the water during the night and turned his searchlight up into the sky so the Cecil J. Doyle (DE-368) could find us. The ship came right over and began picking us up."

Had things not been so desperate at that point, they might have been comical, as the raft was filling up quickly with survivors struggling to stay in them. Eugene explained, "So they picked me up, then we went and got the other two guys. Now there's six of us on this raft. It's getting pretty crowded but we run onto three other guys and we picked them up. Now there's nine of us on this little raft. It's just about dark and figure we'll make it through the night one way or another." Marks explained his own struggle over what to do next: "We would have to make heartbreaking decisions. I decided that the men in groups stood the best chance of survival. They could look after one another, could splash and scare away the sharks and could lend one another moral support and encouragement. … Even though we were near the equator, the wind whipped up. We had long since dispensed the last drop of water, and scores of badly injured men were softly crying with thirst and with pain. And then, far out on the horizon, there was a light."

With that much done, it seemed that there was little else that could be accomplished before a ship arrived to pick up the remaining survivors, but the rescue efforts continued. "At dark, the engines were cut and a sea anchor streamed. After darkness, several shouts for help were heard nearby. Roland A. Shepard ARM3c and Warren A. Kirchoff S1c volunteered to go out in a rubber raft and try to locate these men. They were successful in rescuing 2 more men. Meanwhile, 1st Lt. Richard C. Alcorn of the 4th Emergency Rescue Squadron had arrived from Peleliu and made an open sea landing just before dark near Lt. Marks. Also, Lt. Frank J. LeBlanc of VPB-23 arrived and found the 2 planes on the water. After dropping survival equipment to survivors who fired red Very Flares, Lt. LeBlanc circled the two amphibians that were on the water and marked them with a flare when the first rescue vessel, the CECIL J DOYLE DE-368, came into view."

DE-368 USS Cecil J. Doyle

Picture of the USS *Cecil J. Doyle*

Eugene later wrote, "About midnight, a little bit before there was a light shining off of the bottom of the cloud and we knew then we were saved. That was the spotlight of the Cecil Doyle. The Navy is on the scene. There's a ship comin'. You can't believe how happy we were, guys screamin' and yellin', 'We're saved, We're saved.'" In his detailed account, Haynes recorded that the "Cecil J. Doyle had a big net down over the side. Some of the sailors came down the side of the netting and pulled our rafts alongside. They put a rope around me; we were too weak to climb up. When they tried to grab hold of me I remember saying, "I can get up!" But I couldn't. Two sailors dragged me down the passageway. By the wardroom pantry, someone gave me a glass of water with a mark on it and would only give me so much water. I drank and when I asked for more, he said that was all I could have this time. Then the skipper asked me what ship I was from. I told him we were what was left of the Indianapolis."

Around the same time, Cox was also being rescued. "The next thing I remember was a bright light shining in my face, and a strong arm pulling me into a little boat and taking me to the USS Bassett. I still had enough strength, with a little help, to climb a rope ladder. I got on the deck, took two steps and fell on my face. Someone picked me up and carried me to a bunk - a canvas covered bunk. They laid me face down, with my hands under me and I fell asleep. I don't know how long it was before I woke up, but when I did I realized that my hands were stuck to the canvas. When I rolled over it nearly pulled my hide off. … Two sailors from the Bassett took me and washed me down and tried to get the oil of me. I had sores all over me, they looked just like burns and the hide was coming off. They took tweezers and took strips of skin off my shoulders from where my life jacket had been. I lost all my body hair and I lost my fingernails and toenails. I had basically been pickled in salt water."

In his account of that night, one of the rescuers wrote, "The DOYLE arrived near the 2 planes at 0015 and at once dispatched a motor whaleboat, doctor and first aid party. Transfer of the 56 injured and weak survivors from Lt. Marks plane to the DOYLE began at 0045 and was completed about 0330 on August 3 Because of the damage done to the PBY-5A by the DOYLE's whaleboat and the survivors themselves, it was decided not to attempt a takeoff and to scuttle the aircraft. As such, PBY-5A 46472 was sunk by 40 mm shellfire from the DOYLE at 0800. Lt Alcorn of the 4th ERS after transferring his one survivor to the DOYLE, took-off at 0730 and returned to Peleliu. Lt JG Maurice D. Launders of VPB-23 and LCDR Max V. Ricketts CO of VPB-23 took off at 0055 & 0725 respectively 3 August to relieve Lts . Marks and LeBlanc . Lt JG Launders arrived on station at 0345 and could see the DOYLE picking up survivors using searchlights. He circled until daylight (0630) then started to search in front of 4 surface ships which had by then arrived. Dropping smoke floats on every possible lead to survivors, such as rafts, bodies, boxes and debris, Lt JG Launders directed the surface craft to at least 2 survivors and 2 bodies. LCDR. Ricketts relieved him on station at 0915 and continued search for survivors. Detecting the tiny flash of a mirror, he found 2 life-rafts containing 9 survivors. He summoned the RINGNESS APD-100 which picked them up. Lt. C. E. Mykland of VPB-23 also took off at 1526 but by the time he reached the scene it was dark. He landed at Peleliu having come from Ulithi. From 4 to 8 August, the search for survivors was continued but no additional survivors were found alive after the morning of 3 August. The searches yielded only bodies and debris. 91 bodies were located by planes and buried at sea by surface vessels."

The destroyer USS *Helm* took part in the rescue and salvage efforts

The destroyer USS *Madison* took part in the rescue and salvage efforts

The destroyer USS *Ralph Tabot* took part in the rescue and salvage efforts

Chapter 8: What a Happy Day

"It was daylight the next morning that he came along side us in our little raft. Boy, what a happy day that was to get my feet on the deck again. We got on deck and saluted the officer of the day and asked permission to come aboard, which was Navy tradition. All I had on was my boatson pipe hanging around my neck on a lanyard and I pulled it off and gave it to one of these guys. Why? I don't know, just happy to give anything I owned for bein' rescued, I guess. Anyway, they gave me one spoonful of sweetened water and assigned a guy to me to get me cleaned up because we were all covered with oil. Had been oily for a day, which was a blessing. Had we not had the oil on us like we did, the sun would have really ruined us. It was a good thing we had the oil on." - Woody Eugene

Once they were aboard the USS *Cecil J. Doyle*, each of the survivors was ministered to according to his needs, and Eugene explained how the experience even affected that process: "So I went to the shower and got cleaned up as best as I could. I asked the guy, 'Is this fresh water shower or salt water?' He said, 'Fresh water.' I turned my head up to it and opened my mouth and I tried to drink that shower dry. Got off what we could, junk off of me and they gave us clothes, dungarees of course, and found us a bed. All the crew was just the nicest people in the world. They gave up their beds and everything. I went to sleep laying on my back. Unbeknownst to me I noticed when I was showering that my legs were burned. Both legs were burned in the back, halfway between the thigh and the knee to halfway between the knee and the ankle. I went to sleep and didn't see the doctor. They had one doctor aboard and a couple of quartermen but they had more important things to do than take care of me. There was a lot of people in worse shape than I was but they tried to help. I went to sleep, I don't know how long I slept. I went to sleep with my knees drawed up in the bed on my back. I waked up and all that burn had matted together and I couldn't straighten my legs so I spent the rest of my time until I got aboard the hospital ship on a stretcher. They wanted to move me around so they put me on a stretcher."

Haynes found himself in the unique position of being a patient rather than a physician: "The next thing I knew, I was sitting in a shower. I remember corpsmen or seamen cleaning off my wounds, trying to wash the oil from me and dress my burns. I remember trying to lick the water coming down from the shower. They put me in a bunk and I passed out for about 12 hours. I recall the first bowel movement I had after I was picked up, I passed fuel oil. The other fellows found the same thing. The Cecil J. Doyle took us to Peleliu. We were taken ashore and put into hospital bunks. I remember they came in and got our vital statistics -- we had discarded our dog tags because they were heavy. They changed our dressings. Some of the men got IV's [intravenous solution], though I didn't, While there I began to eat a little and get some strength back."

A few days later, the men were transferred to a medically equipped vessel, and it was here that Eugene began to get the care he really needed. "Got aboard the hospital ship and three days later, my legs are still bent and matted together. I remember going aboard the hospital ship. They hoisted us aboard and I was still on the stretcher. The doctor was standing on the deck directing traffic, this one goes to the emergency room and this one goes to the ward and it got to me and he sent me to the emergency room. I got in there and they laid me on the operating table on my stomach and started to give me a shot. I said, 'Doc, no shot, it ain't a goin' to hurt any worse than it hurts already so if you got something to do, you do it.' The doc said, 'Do it to you son'?, and the nurse handed me a folded up towel, a wet towel and said, 'You better hang on to this.' The doctor put one hand on my ankle, one hand on my buttocks and straightened my leg and I thought my head would go through the roof and as weak as I was I just about twisted that towel in two. Then he did the same thing to the other leg and they picked all of the scab off with tweezers, laid gauze on it and put some kind of ointment on it and it stayed that way."

Despite the pain, Eugene was still grateful for the care he received decades later. "They changed it every few hours and put stuff on it again. This was in the mornin' before noon. Then we spent the rest of that day and that night and the next day and the next night aboard the Tranquility. We got into Guam to a Naval Hospital. They transferred us off of the ship over to the hospital. We was there for five weeks or so and they would tweezer my legs and put gauze and ointment on several times. To this day, I don't know what they used on it but I have no scars. On the back of one leg I have a scar that is maybe an inch long. That's the only thing I have from it. They finally discharged us all from the hospital. They kept us all in the hospital, the whole crew until everybody was able to move out. Then they moved us down to what they call the submarine R & R camp. We thought we'd died and gone to heaven. This is not the Navy. You go to bed when you want and get up when you want. You go over to the kitchen and tell the cook what you want to eat and how you want it fixed, like downtown a café. Well I was discharged on the 3rd day of December 45 and that was the end of my Navy career."

Survivors of the *Indianapolis* being treated on Guam

For his part, Dr. Haynes soon learned that he had duties to perform, even as he was recovering. In fact, that is why readers today have such a detailed account of the events surrounding the loss of the *Indianapolis*. "Then after 2 or 3 days at Peleliu, someone came in and said that I was going to Guam. The next thing I knew, they hauled me out on a stretcher and onto a hospital ship. The commanding officer of the ship, a friend of mine, was Bart [Bartholomew, Surgeon General of the Navy, 1955-1959] Hogan. Bart came in and said, 'I know you don't feel well but you're going to have to go before the Inspector General. I'm going to send a corpsman in and I want you to start at the beginning and dictate everything you can remember about what happened because as time goes on you're going to forget and things are going to change.' So I sat down and dictated off and on for 3 days on the way to Guam. When I'd get tired I'd fall asleep and then I'd wake up and he'd come back. When we landed, Bart gave me a copy of what I dictated and I took it when I went to the Inspector General's office. I told my story, answered their questions, and gave them this report unedited, saying, 'Here it is. This is probably as accurate as I can be.' And that document is the file at the Inspector General's office. All the people who wrote books about the Indianapolis used it."

This was necessary in part because the Navy was investigating the sinking and the loss of nearly 900 men. Ultimately, the Navy court-martialed McVay, and out of nearly 400 ships lost by the Navy during the war, McVay was the only captain to face a court-martial. The Navy reported, "He was acquitted of failure to give timely orders to abandon ship. He was found guilty of negligence in not causing a zigzag to be steered. He was sentenced to lose one hundred numbers in his temporary grade of Captain and also in his permanent grade of Commander. The Court and also the Commander in Chief, United States Fleet recommended clemency. The Secretary of the Navy has approved these recommendations, remitted the sentence, and restored Captain McVay to duty."

McVay discussing the sinking of the ship with war correspondents in Guam

In spite of what it might have considered leniency by allowing him to remain on duty, the Navy's sentence all but spelled the end of McVay's career, and he never recovered from the sense that he had the blood of his men on his hands. After suffering through a spate of mental health problems, McVay committed suicide in 1968. For their part, his surviving crewmen never held him accountable for any deaths and fought for decades to clear his name. McVay also had an unusual defender in Hashimoto, the commander of I-58, who participated in the efforts to exonerate McVay. In 1999, the Japanese commander wrote a letter to Congress insisting that I-58 would have hit the *Indianapolis* even if McVay had ordered the ship to zigzag. "I would have been able to launch a successful torpedo attack against his ship whether it had been zigzagging or not...Our peoples have forgiven each other for that terrible war and its consequences. Perhaps it is time your peoples forgave Captain McVay for the humiliation of his unjust conviction.

In October 2000, the same month Hashimoto died, Congress passed legislation to exonerate McVay, and President Bill Clinton signed it. By the summer of 2001, McVay's record had been cleared of all wrongdoing.

The USS *Indianapolis* National Memorial in Indianapolis, IN

Bibliography

Bauer, Karl Jack; Roberts, Stephen S. (1991), *Register of Ships of the U.S. Navy, 1775–1990: Major Combatants*, Westport, Connecticut: Greenwood Press.

Miller, David M. O. (2001), *Illustrated Directory of Warships of the World*, New York City: Zenith Press.

Silverstone, Paul (2007), *The Navy of World War II, 1922–1947*, New York City: Routledge.

"The Sinking of USS Indianapolis: Navy Department Press Release, Narrative of the Circumstances of the Loss of USS Indianapolis, 23 February 1946". U.S. Navy. 23 February 1946. Retrieved 2015-02-02.

Stille, Mark (2009), *USN Cruiser vs IJN Cruiser: Guadalcanal 1942*, Oxford, United Kingdom: Osprey Publishing.

Made in the USA
Las Vegas, NV
07 September 2023